WIDE AWAKE IN SOMEONE ELSE'S DREAM

WIDE AWAKE
IN SOMEONE ELSE'S
DREAM

POEMS BY
M. L. LIEBLER

WAYNE STATE UNIVERSITY PRESS   DETROIT

12 11 10 09 08   5 4 3 2 1

Library of Congress Cataloging-in-Publication Data

Liebler, M. L.
Wide awake in someone else's dream : poems / by M. L. Liebler.
p. cm. — (Made in Michigan writers series)
ISBN-13: 978-0-8143-3382-2 (pbk. : alk. paper)
ISBN-10: 0-8143-3382-6 (pbk. : alk. paper)
I. Title.
PS3562.I4418W53 2008
811'.54—dc22
2007029901

michigan council for
arts and cultural affairs

This book is supported by the Michigan Council for Arts and Cultural Affairs

Grateful acknowledgment is made to the DeRoy Testamentary Foundation for the
support of the Made in Michigan Writers Series.

Lyrics from "Between the Ground and God" by Stewart Francke, from the album *House of
Lights* on Blue Boundary Records © 1997. Reprinted by kind permission of the author.

Excerpt from "The Moment I Knew My Life Had Changed" by Maria Mazziotti Gillan, from
Things My Mother Told Me © 2000, Guernica Editions. Reprinted by kind permission of the
author.

Lyrics from "Gethsemane" by Ricki Lee Jones, from the album *The Sermon on Exposition
Boulevard* on New West Records © 2007, The Words Group Music (ASCAP). Reprinted by kind
permission of Ricki Lee Jones and Lee Cantelon.

Excerpt from "Stigma" © 2007 by D. H. Melham, from *Stigma* & *The Cave*. Syracuse University
Press, 2007. Reprinted by kind permission of the author.

Excerpt from "Against Death" © 2007 by Gary Metras. Reprinted by kind permission of the
author.

∞

Designed and typeset by Maya Rhodes
Composed in Copperplate Gothic and Clifford

For Gary Metras,
who taught me the wonders
of this world and this life

And for Aunt Jim and Uncle Earl Ensroth,
who often gave me shelter from the storm
all those years ago

CONTENTS

IT WAS NOT UNTIL LATER
THAT I KNEW, RECOGNIZED THE MOMENT
FOR WHAT IT WAS, MY LIFE BEFORE IT,
A GRAY LANDSCAPE, SHAPELESS AND MISTY;
MY LIFE AFTER, FLOWERING FULL AND LEAFY
AS THE CHERRY TREES THAT ONLY TODAY
HAVE TORN INTO BLOOM.

—MARIA MAZZIOTTI GILLAN,
"THE MOMENT I KNEW MY LIFE HAD CHANGED"

MEMORIES HUDDLE LIKE FUGITIVES.

—D. H. MELHEM, "STIGMA"

I

BLUE ALONE IN RED SQUARE
THE RUSSIA POEMS

Я помню чудное мгновенье:
Передо мной явилась ты,
Как мимолетное виденье,
Как гений чистой красоты.

I REMEMBER A WONDERFUL MOMENT
AS BEFORE MY EYES YOU APPEARED,
LIKE A VISION, FLEETING, MOMENTARY,
LIKE A SPIRIT OF THE PUREST BEAUTY.

—ALEKSANDR PUSHKIN, "TO A. P. KERN"

THE LETTING GO

Little by little
It starts. In Siberia,
I see a reflection—
Myself standing still
In the afternoon shadow
Of ancient Russia.
I know now what
I have never realized
Before. I am alone

In darkness—a shade
Of myself here
On another cold
Siberian sidewalk,
So many miles away
From Moscow,
And even further
From myself. Still,

I find songs in this
Old world, as I gather
My ragged spirit in mid-
May and struggle
To dance away from what is
Hidden in snow beyond
This here and now.

HERMITAGE

Inside this Russian Ark
Two of everything, at least,
From Rembrandt to Van Gogh

And all the Western greats.
Here, in the very heart
Of St. Petersburg, history
Embraces everyday life
Written with blood—
Old victories and
That one good fight
On the frontier of justice.

And the Russian bear sleeps
Close to the ground,
Listening to a world moving
Outside its bruised rib cage.

MOTHER VOLGA

In the Siberian
Tundra, cemeteries
Are brickyard gardens.

Tomorrow, the framers will again
Awake in snow and melting
Rain. Rosseya! Hidden
Giant in the backyard,
I hear you singing

With lost nationalism.
Along the mighty Volga,
Men bow and take off
fur hats to salute your past.

ZHILLI BILLI
(Once Upon a Time)

The Russian flag atop
The House of Scientists,
In downtown Novosibirsk,
Has become my Dog Star.

Each morning under
The bright Siberian sun,
I rise, yawn, and center
My soul to set my heart's

Compass. In my dreams,
Sometimes, I think I see
Pushkin's tigers in the night-
Time of lost fairy tales.

They are half asleep
And waiting as they
Whisper
"Zhilli Billi!"

PRAGUE SPRING

In the dark green
Winding paths of Stromovka
Park, I am buried in flowers.
Another Prague spring—
Eastern European stillness
Falls from the ancient
Hardwoods as a breeze shadows
Yesterday's iron and metal wind.

On this soft blue pond, one
White rose spins under
A May sun broken only
By winds that sift
The tall trees
On history's angels.

To the east,
The moving waters
Of the Vlata River,
Its current taking
My name downstream past
Red-throated blackbirds chirping
Another language I will never know.

Within the silence of morning,
I listen to distant whispers
Of Communism, and I think maybe
This is the real plot to the story
Of my life. Momentarily, I sit
On the bank, alone in Stromovka Park,
Listening for an echo to whisper
How the tale will end.

BLUE ALONE IN RED SQUARE

I sit blue alone
In Red Square: Moscow—

Nearly 90 years after
The Bolshevik Revolution

And 13 years from old
Communism; the way it was,

The way it is.
And while things change,

Others are clearly the same—
My problem is trying

To distinguish between
The two. In this still

Red place, ambiguity
Melds into daily life.

For Irena—Girl in Siberia

I am taking back from Russia
A young girl's poem
Written in the sadness
Of a gray university classroom.

Through a slow Siberian rain,
She wrote, "A young man dreams
To escape the desperate overcoat
Of his too young country."

On the streets of Siberia,
Soft wind pricks
Hard at all these gentle faces—

Hungry people moving
Through the emptiness
Of a sad moon that hangs

Alone above the old House of Scientists
On Morskoy Prospekt.
Finally, I gather her poems up,

Tell her I will take them all
To America where they will live.
And I remember her—

A young student who cried,
In the dark lines of her poetry,
"I want to live forever,
But I can't bear my own mind
Here in this cold, cold distance,
Away from everyone and everywhere."

I tell her it's only a train ride—easy—
To Moscow, but she doesn't have the ruble,
And time is not kind to those who wait.

I Once Refused to Change

Finding my way here
In the darkness is
Like being a man who refuses
To change his life
Because he fears what
It might become.

In the end, this healing
Leaves only soft scars
Against a dark night of stars,
Sickles, and blazing red hammers.

THE BLACK HEART OF COMMUNISM

Their dreams are
The national nightmare.
The Russian heart is hidden

Beneath the rubble of old cars,
Trash cans, garbage blues
In the alleys of yesterday's
Ideologies and charmed deceptions.

I heard this rumor yesterday—Lenin died
Holding his head in his hands
As if his ideas were too heavy
For this world. And in Siberia

They say that Stalin died—
His heart the color of mud
At the bottom of the Black Sea.

Russia is the scar of Europe.
A long, tight cut right down
The middle of its once vibrant soul.

When America thought
It had won the Russians'
Hearts and minds, America never
Realized—it had neither.

For decades we battled against
Their country only to find more
Similarities than differences. In their eyes,

A history as long as the Volga
And as deep as the world.
Together we have battled, and
Together we have struggled,

And at the end of the long
Century, America was only
Treading the waters of hatred
In oceans of lies—our own

Anger and misunderstanding flowing
Through selfish foolishness,

Ideals, and wasted opportunities.
Now, everyone knows that we are

The same. It took decades to discover
What we should have long already known.

SUNSET OVER ST. PETERSBURG

People move through their lives
In the streets of Petrograd;
Another giant of human spirit
Crawling half awake through

Years of poverty and war,
An unholy strife—translated to history
With so many blue stories in this
Old collectivist dream. There

Has always been heart
In the workers of Russia—
Their anxiety moving by metro from Lenin
Plochad toward the Motherland

Where Lenin once struggled
On the corner of the sun
That today slides behind
The clouds and the gold-
Plated roofs of Peterhoff Palace.

II

GERMANY IS THE BROKEN HEART

THE GERMANY POEMS

IN THE THIRD-CLASS SEAT SAT THE JOURNEYING BOY,
AND THE ROOF-LAMP'S OILY FLAME
PLAYED DOWN ON HIS LISTLESS FORM AND FACE,
BEWRAPT PAST KNOWING TO WHAT HE WAS GOING,
OR WHENCE HE CAME.

—THOMAS HARDY, "MIDNIGHT ON THE GREAT WESTERN"

FROM THE GATHERING HILLS
OF STUTTGART

The broken sun's
Light slides slowly through
The window of this apartment
On Charlottenstrasse. I see
The ghosts of my family
Coming down from
The hills above Stuttgart.

It seems like clouds gathering
Above, but when I look again, it is
My grandmother, filled with love,
the one who raised me from birth,
And to her right my grandpa
Greeting me on the streets of Baden-
Württemberg.

Is this where they all have gone?
Back to the homeland. This is
Our old neighborhood. Germany
Is the broken heart I have
Never forgotten. The origin
Of who I am. I have come
Home to my beginnings,
And my family has waited
For my return from an America
That I never really knew.

SITTING WITH MY MOTHER IN MUNICH

We are ghosts together
Under this warm German sun
On a Sunday afternoon
In Munich—Just up the narrow
Street from Kreuzkirche
Near Marian Platz
Just before worship.
We sit and pray
And laugh about
Everything that once was.

She speaks softly
Over coffee mit slagsana,
And I hear all the stories
Of the way
It used to be
Back in the golden Germany
Of her past. A place
She never really knew,
But somehow we both feel
As through we are finally
Home in this world.

She leans over and touches
My forehead and then my arm.

I feel her soft breath, angels
Moving through the fine hairs
On my arm. "Yes, Mom,"
I say, "It's like we never left.
We have always been
Here near the Marian Platz
On such a day in this sweet
City." For us, what
Else is possible?

ALONE, INSIDE MY HEART

I am listening to the church
Inside my heart, alone
On the river's bank

Where I long for soft wind
To bend around my knees
With all the glory of this life.

I want to meditate upon
These trees that line the avenues
In the city of my forefathers. Stuttgart,

I stand alone in your shadow.
Once I was tired and broken.
Now, I find I am here,

Comforted in the house
Of my birth within
The tender heart of my life.

FLOWING LIKE THE RHINE

Today is one more
Day to reconsider
The rooms of my life
And to change where
They all lead. I feel
My soul, upstream, moving
As the Rhine flows
Through my heart.

Somewhere between Mainz
And Koblenz, I understand
These true green waters
That touch along each shore-
Line northward from where
I last remember my life
Full as a June moon over
The wine-sweet Rhineland

Valley through Moselle and Saar,
Where I look for all the broken pieces
Of my past, the ancestors
Of old Germany—centuries move
In this old river's flow.
How can time now matter?

I sleep on a quiet river-
Bank where the moon is
The soul-shine of my past.

THREAD

How could I have ever known
Before that it would take me
Down old cobblestone streets
In ancient Munich?

In this place, old spirits
Were raised. I was Bavarian,
One hundred years ago. Somehow
There is life embedded here in the

Mortar between these bricks. I keep
Looking back for that one small piece
Of stone that is the future.

In Heidelberg

In Heidelberg, I walk in the darkness
Of the old Schloss dungeon.
I am looking for my life
Among the broken bones and stones
In the ruins of my own history,
And within the quietness of myself.

I think there might be buried here,
In Heidelberg, a story for me
To rebuild my life. Here,
Underneath this rubble and darkness—
Free from all wars.

We're all just water passing
Through like this old river
          In Heidelberg.

Dachau Death Morning Blues

> First they came for the Jews
> and I did not speak out
> —Pastor Martin Niemöller

Death came alongside me and brought
Me through the workers' gate.
Inside the camp, a lonely woman's shadow
Follows me, whispering into my deaf ear
All the horrors still burning
In the forest of the German night.

Between the turning gears,
A human factory of skin
Pulled tight over the heavy pounding
Of pain and steel. I meet people
Who speak across this barren,
Cold November yard.

They whisper to my heart,
"Please—do not let them forget
Our hungry spirits. Don't forget
Us here in your fading memories
Of democracy and peace!"

MOVING WITH THE GHOSTS
OF HISTORY: STUTTGART

It's 5:00 a.m. in America,
And most people are asleep
As I travel in the dark slumber
Of dreams on another continent
Unaware of all the moving ghosts,
Stirring and shaping the news
That will become tomorrow.

North winds are always cold
And harsh as I slide up the rails
From Stuttgart to Berlin. I know
The busy people don't think
I can see them talking
Out the train window,
Behind the barns,
In the fields,
Over their fresh crops
in Baden-Württemberg.

But I know these ghosts,
Climbing through the slow history
Of my blood. And now I am
One with their brittle bones, attempting
To conquer the weaknesses in this world.

III

THE TINY BIRDS OF ISRAEL

THE JERUSALEM POEMS

NOW WE WENT UP TO THE GARDEN
BENEATH THE OLIVE TREE
THE BELLS WERE RINGING
THE ROOSTER CROWS . . .

YOU KNOW YOU WAKE UP ONE MORNING
AND YOU'RE SOMEONE ELSE
YOU'RE ON YOUR OWN
THERE IS NO MIRACLE TO TAKE YOU HOME
　　—RICKIE LEE JONES, "GETHSEMANE"

LONG MAY THE SPIRITS INCARNATE THE SONGS OF BIRDS
AS THE SUN RESONATES ITS LIGHT THROUGH AIR.
LONG MAY THE SPIRITS FLY IN THE RIOT OF BIRD SONG
WHEN THE EARTH TILTS TOWARD ABUNDANCE AND
　　BEYOND.
THOUGH THE SONGLESS DEAD OUTNUMBER
THOSE WHO SING, STILL, EACH BIRD HAS A SONG.
　　—GARY METRAS, "AGAINST DEATH"

THE TINY BIRDS OF ISRAEL

Articulate, little bird
Sounds swimming through whispers
Across lawns toward
The northern fields of Nazareth
And up into the dry holes
In the throat of the sun.

On earth, small finches
Bathe in warmth. Tiny
Lungs fill full with
Fresh mountain scents
In bloom in
The Middle-Eastern desert.

Small birds break out
In peace songs from inside
Their gentle hearts.
First, tranquility
Fades into violence.
Time takes them all
Eventually into darkness,
Death, and loss where
They will sing no more.

UNSPOKEN

In Jerusalem,
From Mount Zion,
Sound moves inside
Bending flowers—
New languages.
Unspoken.

Tempered,
Close to a whisper,
Rhythm and soul
As alive as fish

Rising up
Toward the surface
In silence. This water
Is truth under
The old desert sun.

OLD CITY: JERUSALEM AFTER DARK

Through the streets
Of Old Jerusalem,
Moon-heavy spirits
Dance in forgotten dreams
Detaching hope from memories:
Bombs from the north—
Suicide from Gaza in the south.

Follow the sounds
Of war to the edge
Of the Christian Quarter,
The Jewish Quarter,
And the Muslim Quarter.
Everywhere love is a faint murmur

From the deserts of different faiths
All sprung from the same source.
Now, a dry well—empty
Within the forgotten
Temples of ourselves.

50 Miles from Beirut—
We Are in Charge
Lines Found in the Jerusalem Post, *July 2006*

This is Israel.
Follow my instructions.
Sternly stop at your
Current positions, and don't
Try to sneak further into Lebanon.

This checkpoint is set up
To protect you from terrorists,
And to further serve our efforts
To pressure their government.
We know this siege is meant
To smuggle captives out of our range.

Our main focus: Hezbollah
And their infrastructure—
We must clear this waiting area
Of revolution and war.

When this war broke out,
They refused to heed
Our orders, but now
The navy has been allowed
To be in charge.
In the lower levels
Of it all—Lies.

SHABBAT ON BEN YEHUDA STREET

In the stillness
Of another Shabbat,
Saturday morning seems as lonely
As the crouching doves
Stretching above on wires
From the walking mall to
The Russian churches, and all the way
To David's tomb. The distance
Is an ellipsis dotting through
The history books of time.

NOTHING WITHIN

Listen, I understand nothing.
I have sat inside away
From this dampness
To keep my soul dry.
Waiting and waiting,
I look for the sun to evaporate
These haunted shadows of rain.

Listen, I am not making this up.
I have no ideas anymore.
I have studied these clouds closely,
Looked deep into each drop of rain,
Prayed for a respite from the weather
Of myself, and all I feel are occasional
Somber breezes. My soul is
Locked in the outside,
Where I keep listening
For my heart's beat.

BROKEN MIRRORS

Angels settle in smoke
Upon the reflections
In broken mirrors.

Moonless mist, cool
In the breeze rising
High above the olive trees,

Wind of rosemary and spice.
This world smolders—just another broken
Heart filled with the burning

Fires of this tortured world.

WEEPING AT THE TOMB

When age surrenders the body,
When the spirit leaves to become
Someone else's memories—
You find the changing seasons:
A brother's forgotten birthday,
Your mother's marriage, a grandmother's
anniversary, all this now a deep ocean
sinking in someone else's heart.

Your messages from the past remain
Lost at the post office like yesterday's
Black and white photographs or old postcards
Lying for years in the mildewed bottom
Of your uncle's old cigar box.
All is memory blowing across
The once blonde hairs of your
Youthful arm. Tomorrow is a ghost

Waiting for you to sit alone
Under a blue moon that willingly
Hangs, again, over old Jerusalem.
You contemplate the place
Where they washed the body
Of Christ with rose water and perfume
Outside His tomb where a church

Now stands. You weep
For time and
You kneel in faith.

THE MEDITERRANEAN NEVER ENTERED
(The Tel Aviv Blues)

When I was a child,
The Mediterranean meant
Nothing to me.

Today, I sit
Alone and alive at its
Shoreline, daydreaming.

I sit in salt
And wind filling my lungs.
The past is lost in baptizing
Waves of silent youth.

BROKEN BREAD

Broken bread
Heals the angels
Of my past.

How many times
Have I eaten
Of the Body?

And how little
Have I really fed
The angels?

Emptiness settles
Like rust
At the bottom
Of our hearts.

I am as broken as bread.
I am more whole than ever.

EVANGELINE, THE GHOST
(Sitting in Jerusalem Thinking about New Orleans)

Under humidity and moss
In the sweat of Evangeline,
Ghosts slip out from cracks

In the sidewalks of Storyville.
Together they huddle on Iberville
Street with dark secrets of the Mississippi

Sliding over broken levees
Swallowing hearts, spirits awash in waves
Moving in reverse toward the Gulf.

They will settle
To the bottom—salty
Bones in another Middle Passage.

This humidity is rising
Up across America—
Shadows hiding our ancestors:

While broken bodies drift and
Lost souls drown again in the old
Lies of familiar darkness.

IV

WIDE AWAKE IN
SOMEONE ELSE'S DREAM

SOON STARS WILL NEST IN THE BROW OF THE TIRED;
A QUIET SIMPLICITY ENTERS COOL CHAMBERS
AND ANGELS STEP SOUNDLESSLY FROM THE BLUE

—GEORG TRAKL, "AUTUMN OF THE LONELY ONE"

WHEN THE LIGHTS GO OUT AND THE HOUSE IS DARK
AND YOU FEEL ALONE, YOU WILL FIND A SPARK

THERE IS A PLACE WHERE I COME FROM
THERE IS A FAITH IN WHAT WE'VE DONE
I WANT TO LIVE BETWEEN THE GROUND AND GOD

—STEWART FRANCKE, "BETWEEN THE GROUND AND GOD"

MAKING IT RIGHT

*(Lines composed after being asked to lecture on labor
in Detroit during the Depression at the Amerika Haus
Lecture Series in Munich, Germany 2004)*

> YOU KNOW WHAT WORK IS——IF YOU'RE
> OLD ENOUGH TO READ THIS YOU KNOW WHAT
> WORK IS, ALTHOUGH YOU MAY NOT DO IT.
> FORGET YOU.
> ——PHILIP LEVINE, "WHAT WORK IS"

I bring no poetry today
From the oil and grease
Soul of my Detroit.

This history I am is
Only, and nothing more,
Than the son of an autoworker.

Just another Detroit man beaten
Down by the tortured years
Of Depression, World Wars,

And the awful angst of unemployment.
This is my story without balance
Weighing heavier on the side

Of heartache and less on the side
Of the sacred and glorious.
This is my story of what no work is

And what it can do to the
Working class in the darkness
Of our desperation.

I wish, now, I did have some
Kind of a poem to say aloud,
Right here—to make you

All understand what is inside
The blackened heart and under
The whittled bones of the people

Who have been left behind
In the ashes of the plant. I guess

I could read you a poem about how labor
Takes a boy and makes him a worker
Before he is allowed to become a man.

How the factory humiliates
And intimidates all people
With endless assembly and useless work.

How the line takes one ounce
Of every soul lived for every
Minute it is sped up to completion.

How Henry Ford's great innovation
Doomed generations to continuous
Monotony in the name of "making a living."

But, I am afraid that I can only bring
The small news of what becomes of people
Who work hard with greasy hands.

About people who learn that their reality is
Having their names spelled out in factory
Smoke long before they were born. A birthright

For workers to endure through
The long loneliness of industry
And unemployment lines where

We wait and wait for our
Bread and roses to fall from the sky
Like beads of perspiration upon our graves.

We dream that, maybe, prosperity
Is really just around the corner. So we
get up every morning with hope, and

We return each night to the broken houses
Of our lives, seldom realizing that it is our
Labor that keeps this whole world together.

I guess, in the end, we do not know
What work is, but still we continue to
Do it over and over, making it right.

Bitter Tea—The Muddy Passaic

I drink the bitter tea
From the bottom of the empty
Soul of the muddy Passaic River
Under the Great Falls in Paterson,
New Jersey, where the dark water
Meets the riverbed of reality. I turn

Toward God inside the Blessed
Sacrament Church to pray over
The history of the shattered, abandoned,
And broken ghosts of the workers that I
See in their faded reflections through the
Scarred windows of the old Colt Gun Mill;

The lost lives of Paterson's working
Class. There is little antidote now
For the hunger and emptiness
Of unemployment. All the rivers
Of this broken world could never
Fill the gap when jobs like these

Dry up the muddy waters. Suffering,
Doubt, and loss become the mill town's
Nightmare: "No Help Wanted!" Today,

I sit with all the others,
Head in hands, along the closed
Banks of the once mighty Passaic
Waiting and waiting for our new day
To rise up and take us all downstream
With those dark river currents to a new
America of time and hope, where we will
Again sing to remember our history with the
Old, familiar tunes of work and faith.

OUTSOURCING

I had an idea recently. "Genius!"
I thought. I would disassemble the factory
Of myself, break it all down and
Ship the most valuable parts to
Some other places. To do this, I had
To carefully detach each wire
And bolt, and secretly unscrew me
From me, as not to grab anyone's
Attention or curiosity. For example,
While my foot was asleep, I sent
All of my memories south. While
My scalp prickled with beads of sweat,
I sent my love north to cool, and later,
While my brain was entranced with
Commercials on television, I sent those
Mysterious 21 grams of my soul, which I
Read about in *Time* magazine, straight
Out of this world—Way further than Mexico,
China, Pakistan, or anywhere anyone has ever
Heard of. Gone—Vanished—just like that!

When all was said and done, very little
Of the old me was left. Yes, I had my
Ever-growing fingernails and toenails,
The occasional annoying hidden body rashes

Here and there, and of course plenty of those
Middle-aged hairs growing in my ears and
    nose.
But the substance? What was the substance
    anyway?

Suddenly it occurred to me the other day
That when I gave all of me away, what
Remained was just another abandoned factory,
And that's no way to run a life—

ON THE SCRAP

COME TAKE A LITTLE TRIP WITH ME IN 1913
TO CALUMET, MICHIGAN, IN THE COPPER COUNTRY.
—WOODY GUTHRIE, "1913 MASSACRE"

In a small, big town 1913
    At the northernmost reaches
    Of America—sticking out
        Into the cold, deep waters
        Of Lake Superior—beautiful
        Body of lake and fresh earth
        Packed heavy with whitefish and
            copper
    Land, veins mined by immigrants:
Croatia, Hungry, Finland, England.

American multiculturalism
    Long before the academy labeled people
        Through their longitudinal studies
            and statistics.
        Here, in Michigan, the working
            class
        Once again defined the country's
            future by building
        A firm foundation: Keweenaw
            County—just another place

Where labor awakened to confront
business
Owners who were determined
To keep workers enslaved, endangered, and
under

Control. When the first cry of "union" sprung
From the workers' wintry lips as they
stood upon the frozen-
cold streets, the mine owners'
mantra was loud and clear
The managers' chant of
"We'll let the grass grow on your
streets
Before we concede to the
uncivilized
Working class," was an offense to the few
who

Understood English. Those words were met
with
A reckoning response from labor
everywhere.
Fortunately for the mining men of
Calumet
There was a strong-willed woman
Who refused to let injustice

        trample
        Her community down to ash in the
        name of
"Business as usual!"

During the Great Mining Strike of 1913, Big
    Annie
        Clemec of Calumet stood up to be
            counted,
        And she took on the mine owners
            by challenging
        them to "Kill me! Run your
            bayonets and sabers
        Through this flag and kill me! For I
            will not
    Be moved. If this American flag will not
Protect me, then I will die holding it."

Sweet Annie Clemec, Eastern European angel
    of the mines—
    Tall, beautiful Upper Peninsula woman of
        integrity,
        Who marched daily through
        The copper-rich streets of Calumet
            with her American
        Flag raised, stars, red, blue, and
            white,

High above her flowing brown
hair,
Encouraging other men, women, and
children to stand
Together for union and for their fair share.

Big Annie—Lady of Calumet—marched
Head on into the Federal Militia who
watched her
From horsebacks with their silver
sabers drawn
And ready to knock her flag of
freedom from her
Steady hand, but Annie marched
forward, always,
Spitting on the yellow-bellied
soldiers who dared
To take the working man's birthright of
fair
Pay for an honest day.

The miners wanted to work
A little less and spend a little more
time
With their families—The miners
wanted
To be safer in the dark dungeon

Mines webbed with the evil sound
of the widow-maker drill;

In the end, the company won the Strike of 1913
            In Copper County, Michigan. They
                broke the back
            Of labor in their typical, hurtful,
                murdering way
            When they planted a scab-snitch
in the old Italian Hall on Main Street—

December 24th at Big Annie's Christmas party
            For the penniless children
            And the families of the striking
                men. As gifts
            Of oranges, handmade dolls,
                clothes, and such
            Were passed to the children from
                Santa on the stage,
A loud cry of "Fire! Fire!" rose up over the
    heads of the children
And the frantic strikers. A cloud of panic hung
    like a noose

Over the people who scrambled toward the one
    and only door.
A human stampede where body after body

piled up on the stairway out.
　　When calm was restored,
　　　　　　74 people, mostly children, lay
　　　　　　　　buried in a twisted heap
　　　　　　Of bones, blood, skin, and hair. A
　　　　　　　　Working-Class
　　　　　　Nightmare in the Home of the
　　　　　　　　Brave. All
　　　　　　Brought on by another nameless
　　　　　　　　company snitch
　　　　Who yelled "fire" from his stool-pigeon
　　　　　　perch,
And was never seen again in Calumet City.
　　So—Big Annie picked up

Her flag, one more time, to bury the dead
　　children in the frozen land—
　　　　December 28, 1913. She lead the funeral
　　　　　　procession
　　　　　　　　To their snow-covered graves.
　　　　　　　　The Calumet newspapers reported
　　　　　　　　　　that miners won
　　　　　　　　Nothing of significance during the
　　　　　　　　　　Great Strike.
　　　　　　　　They went back to work without
　　　　　　　　　　their babies,
　　　　Without a raise, without better working

conditions, and without
Recognition for their union. All of that
was buried
In 1913 in the cold Michigan earth.

THE LONELINESS OF A SHADOW

I am sleeping
In a meadow
In this green world.

Dreaming, I fall
Into black
And white photos—

Motionless and asleep.
In this picture, a
Background creek rises

Along the shadow
Of a shoreline traced in
The chalk ghost of myself.

WALKING WITH SUN YET SEN

Along the boulevard
On Tiapa Island
In Macau, and under
The smell of orchards
And spring bloom, I walk
With rebellion in my blood.

Here, along this boulevard,
Named after the great leader
Dr. Sun Yet Sen, I feel
The swiftness of change, and I
Understand its necessity.

Soon after revolution rages
In the clouds above
The bones of today,
A vast change builds
Upon the rest of our
One thousand tomorrows.

THE FINGERTIPS OF NIGHT

Where are my dreams now?
Long ago I remember they danced
Out to the fingertips of night.
Alone in their own enchantment—
In wonder, in the moonlight,
In a universe, I once dreamt
About the truths that hide
Behind the skin of youth.

Now, at midnight—crossing, somewhere
In the middle of my life—there is
A balance. I paint these words
In sleep and pain upon
The back fences of my sadness:

"Never once did I dream
More than I could hold
In the cupped hands
Of youth."

Now, in these later years,
I am, again, close to my
Mother's heart. I

Drive on through lessons,
Sequestered in the darkness, and
I wonder what codes the beating
Heart will send to the blood buried
In the blueness of my veins.

RECONSIDERING THE ROOM

Inside
The
Heart

Shadows
Move
In

Drunken
Dark
Blood

Alone
Whispering
Through

Bones
Of
This

World
That
Can

Never
Know
Truth—

The
Green
Leaves

Of
Youth
Form

Deep
Pools
In

This
Life

BRICKS WITHOUT STRAW

I am bricks without straw
Holding fast to the dark
Night of the soul—where
Even quiet whispers
From God thunder through
The weather of my life.

Crowded black clouds of anger
Push against mistrust in this
World, where rain falls
On an otherwise calm day.

Alone in this world, I wait
To awaken from the long loneliness
Of some new life that is
Stretched out across the rest
Of my days. Alive in the free-
Flowing presence of God.

UNDER THE BLOOD SUN,
VENICE CALLS

Sitting under smooth waves of warm
Heat from the purple blood sun
In Venice, I think about all the things

That could come easily
If I could learn to pray
In silence. I want to dream
In calm. I want to trust
In the peace of forgiveness.

So much in this world
I will never know, yet
It might all be buried, up there,
In the whole of the Venice sun.

The Landscape of Thunder

It is colorless in my hands,
Cold to the touch of anything
Less than my soul. There is
Wind inside my graying
Dream clouds—It calls

Me through to the echoes—
The landscape of my heart.
Life now moves in reverse,
Slow strokes, backward against
A backdrop of anxious roses.

A clock tower trembles.
My heart trembles.
Alive, forever, calling
To define this life in shadows.

In Another Universe

Tomorrow the edge will appear
Far off in some distant cry that has been
Cut through wailing cliffs of horizontal
Clouds that lie like smoke
At the ends of our lives.

The clock yawns
At daybreak. Or, God's fire
Starts in the heart
To burn the soul free from sin.

Once I was
A boy before I was
Born, a simple life crawling in
A twilight circle
Where stars sleep
In the minutes of day.

I wonder if all
The anger I have ever felt
Was really just the soul rubbing
Against the blue gun trigger
Of life. Now, I wonder
If it is a lie told
As truth in another
Universe?

SOUL, DECEIT, CRYING

It beats against
My teeth. Big sounds
Pulled from below
The soul. Deceit—
Cries roar out of the lungs,
A new life pink and thrusting from deep
Within the walls of my mother's dreams.

The words were there
Even when I was not, but
I didn't know them enough
To speak. So I chopped
With my tongue, softness
On the roof of my mouth,
Splashing in vowels. A new
Food being pushed up
Like tulips in my throat.

I sit in anger
And wonder which came first—
The word, or thick sounds
Tossed onto a dark floor.

ARCTIC DREAM

Descending through bruised blueness
In the arctic sky, I find
Reality on the solar ice.

In these moments just before
Landing, I am rediscovering
A part of me that has been

Buried deep in the Inupiat
Earth—under these centuries
Of prayers and rituals.

With them, again, I am
A student of this life
Looking for answers

That seem to stretch across
The tundra as far as the eyes
Can see. Out here I

Do not worry about worry.
I learn the ancient art
Of rhythm and balance.

This wind is truth
Changing like the sun
In the midnight sky.

Slowly it reveals new
Horizons sliding through
A sky that never darkens.

THE FRAGRANT BENEDICTION OF LIFE
After Barry Lopez

Today, I sit at the top of the world
Praying for hours in quietness
And blind forgiveness as love heals all.

In the 24-hour daylight,
I can see myself in the natural
Light of my own heart that is

Buried deep in my chest
Shining through my ribs, a cage
Of reality to which I am bound.

Come sweet Lord— show me the light,
Sensation of peace that lies waiting
For the fragrant benediction of life.

The Sun Dancer's Pledge Sonnet

With this rain comes
The running paint—
A slow drizzle down
The tear paths of our faces.

Nature buries us
With each lament—ready
To pull the sun out
From behind the gray clouds

Of earth. Our habit
Is prayer and our
Prayer is this world.

Our job is to bring
Life out of habit, and prayer
From behind the sun.

WHO KNEW ATTACHMENT WAS NOT
For Lisa Rutledge

She was a Buddhist who knew
Attachment was not a part of her
Prayer and meditation cycle. She

Thought about New York from time
To time, but always kept it hidden
In the mirror of her past. Her life—

Driven by everydayness
With the headlights of all time
Glaring into her once-broken

Heart, but she kept a book
Of poetry close to help her
Heal the scattered pain of this world.

Today, she drives to her job
In warmth, and she'll leave
In the cold darkness of night

Where clouds loom like a rosary
Swinging in her Midwestern heart
Where she'll tuck away her mother's

Note to a young daughter. It says,
"We live to live." This is
The evensong of her soul.

FLOORS OF THE WORLD

In stillness,
Hope rings
The garden
Of a young
Boy's heart.
Music climbs
Down from rainbows
To the cold
Floors of his world.

In dreams,
He lassos
Passing clouds
In the darkness
Of his sleep.

Blues for the Lost Days

I remember the lost days of youth.
Days I never counted or cared about.
Moments when everything
Moved slowly like shadows
Across the lawns of our lives.

I remember long, hot summers
Of baseball and tree climbing,
Wanting only to play
Through the summer's dusks into
The long, cool mornings of autumn.

I remember thinking that this
Could be one endless dream.
One after another—
One after another—

PURPLE IN THE GONE DAY

I am holding
Firm to my purple,
Midnight dreams.

This lilac pain
Rising to the top
Of my pink skin.

In darkness, I feel
Purple in the memory
Of my blood. Deep

Into the blue
Veins of yesterday,
Just another gone

Day where I am
Empty in my mood,
Sliced open wide

By purple light
Under the heart
Of the slivered moon.

I hold myself, now,
In darkness and wait
And wait for my heart

To fold itself into
The deepness of sleep.

ACKNOWLEDGMENTS

The author wishes to extended his sincere gratitude to all those who welcomed him into their countries, their homes and their lives on his many trips abroad.

In Russia: Edward Shornik, CEO, YMCA Novosibirsk; Executive and Director of the Educational Center "Smile"; Alexander Mezdrikov and his wife Youlia Mezdrikova; Professor Olga Ryzhkina at Novosibirsk State University; Natalia Zamyatina, YMCA in St. Petersburg; and the Wayne State students who were fellow travelers to Russia in 2005: Rebecca Gramlich, Noah Morgan, and Lucy "In the Sky" Siegfred.

In Germany: Professor Hans Peter Soder and his beautiful family in München, and his excellent staff Sommer Sherrit and Lena Bittle.

In Israel: Professor Karen Alkalay-Gut at Tel Aviv University; Derek, Jackie, Ashleigh, and Jonzie Stein; Linda Slutzky; Alex. N. Daniels, director of the American Center in Jerusalem; Sara Erlanger; Ralph "DJ Mix Master" Amelan; David Ehrlich at the Tmol Shilshom Café; and Dr. Shai Aran and everyone at the American Center Jerusalem's CLASS Program (Civics, Language, and American

Studies Seminar, Department of Education and Cultural Affairs, U.S. Department of State).

Many thanks must go to Director Mark Ferguson and Louise Speed of Wayne State University's Junior Year in Munich Program, Director Kelli Dixon of Study Abroad and Global Programs at Wayne State, Director Jerry Herron and Kevin Rashid of the Wayne State Honors Program, and President Irvin Reid for his support of Wayne State's global mission.

M. L. is extremely grateful to Katheen Zamora who helped prepare this manuscript; to his editor Annie "Oakley" Martin, Kathy Wildfong, and Jane Hoehner at Wayne State University Press; and to his wife Pamela M. Liebler, who held down the home front while he was abroad.

Thank you to the following journals in which some of these poems have previously appeared:

Connecticut Review
    "Dachau Death Morning Blues"
    "Soul, Deceit, Crying"

Cortland Review
(http://www.cortlandreview.com/issue/34/liebler.html)
    "Walking with Sun Yet Sen"
    "The Loneliness of a Shadow"

Hot Metal Press
(http://hotmetalpress.net/Winter2006.html)
    "Evangeline, the Ghost"
    "Weeping at the Tomb"
    "The Tiny Birds of Israel"
    "Old City: Jerusalem after Dark"
    "Unspoken"

Paterson Literary Review:
    "From the Gathering Hills of Stuttgart"
    "Sitting with My Mother in Munich"
    "For Irina—Girl in Siberia"
    "Moving with the Ghosts of History: Stuttgart"

Temenos: An Online Literary Journal of Central Michigan University
    "The Letting Go"
    "Hermitage"
    "Alone, Inside My Heart"
    "The Tiny Birds of Israel"

Third Wednesday Literary Arts Quarterly
    "Hermitage"
    "In Another Universe"

Weathervane: A Journal of Great Lakes Writing
(http://www.theweathervane.org/poetry.htm)
    "Making It Right"
    "On the Scrap"